THAMES SHIPPING

IN THE 1960s AND 1970s

CAMPBELL McCUTCHEON

AMBERLEY

First published 2013

Amberley Publishing
The Hill, Stroud
Gloucestershire, GL5 4EP

www.amberley-books.com

British Library Cataloguing in Publication Data.
A catalogue record for this book is available from the British Library.

ISBN 978 1 84868 285 6

Typeset in 10pt on 12pt Sabon.
Typesetting and Origination by Amberley Publishing.
Printed in the UK.

Contents

Introduction

It is the founding of a harbour that gave London the importance it still holds today as one of Britain's busiest ports. The port can claim a history of over 2,000 years and was no doubt used before Roman times. It was then that the original harbour was built, along what we now know as the Pool of London. For centuries, the port remained there but, by the late eighteenth century, the port extended for eleven miles on either side of the Thames, with 11,500 cranes loading and unloading some 60,000 vessels per annum. The sheer size of London demanded a constant stream of coastal ships, carrying coal, food and other goods into central London.

From Billingsgate to London Bridge, the river teemed with craft and, further down river, shipyards built new vessels for the ever growing trade. But in the nineteenth century, London had grown too large for the harbour to cope with and new facilities were needed. In 1750, around 6,000 coastal vessels used the port, and in 1795, this had doubled to 11,964, with an almost trebling in foreign cargoes from 234,639 tons to 620,845 tons. Despite the size of ships increasing, the overseas trade was huge and plans began to be made to construct new docks.

Plans were made to construct huge wet docks in the three great bends of the Thames but these came to nothing. In 1799, the West India Dock Act saw the construction of a new dock for the West Indian trade, with other docks following soon after. West India Docks opened in 1802, with the East India Docks a year later. London Docks at Wapping followed in 1805, with the Surrey Commercial Docks in 1807, St Katharine's in 1828 and the Royal Victoria Dock in 1855. As ships grew larger, the size of the docks increased and in the 1860s the South West India Dock opened, as did the Millwall Dock. In 1880 came the Royal Albert Dock and, in 1886, Tilbury, some twenty-five miles from central London by water. The last great dock to be built was the King George V Dock, opened in 1921.

During the war, the docks were bombed extensively and much trade moved to Liverpool and Glasgow, but afterwards, it returned for what was a twenty-five year boom period in London's port before a terminal decline set in, with passenger shipping giving way to aircraft and the container revolution for cargo shipping. London's power stations were closed down as a result of Clean Air Acts and the discovery of North Sea gas.

Closures began in the early 1970s as new developments took place further down river at Tilbury, Harwich and Felixstowe and by the 1980s much of the docklands was in decline. A process of regeneration has seen the building of a new financial centre in East London, the conversion of the Surrey Commercial docks into housing and retail and even an airport in the King George V Dock.

Most of the photos on this volume were taken during a period of decline for the Port of London, from the 1960s until the very early 1980s and they give a flavour of the docks as they once were. It was also a time when Britain still ruled the waves, with many ships still registered here. Times were changing and the 1966 Seamens' Strike saw a death knell for many British lines, as they failed to modernise and build new container ships. The images themselves show a dock system under change, with fewer ships and without the hustle and bustle of the immediate post-war years. However, they give us a valuable record of a dock system in decline.

The decline of the docks was rapid, hastened by a series of recessions in the UK and a decline in the country's industrial base. A growing population also saw a need to remove the slum housing of London's docklands and new building was going to take place in the land vacated by the docks as they moved further downstream.

Today, London's docklands are devoid of the masts of ships but the Port of London is as busy as ever. Tilbury is now the closest dock to London in active use and Felixstowe and Harwich have taken over as the main ports, with Felixstowe able to accommodate the largest vessels afloat. Passenger and ferry services have declined, and even in the Docklands, air has taken over from sea as the primary method of foreign travel, with the London City Airport celebrating its first twenty-five years in 2012.

Chapter 1

The Upper River &
Pool of London

The *Esso Reading* tows a barge up the Thames as a Southern Region electrical multiple unit passes over the river on 23 October 1961.

The *Tattershall Castle* was built in 1934 for the London & North Eastern Railway as a ferry across the Humber and was made redundant when the new Humber Bridge was opened. She was sold and berthed close to Hungerford Bridge, where she is shown here on 27 December 1975.

The motor tanker *Batsman* (217 tons, built 1963) passes St Paul's Cathedral on 24 June 1971.

The waterbus *Ford Consul* and the motor yacht *Thurgar* off Millbank on 7 May 1954.

From the early 1820s, pleasure steamers began to make trips down the river taking holiday makers to the coastal resorts of Margate, Ramsgate, Southend and Clacton. Along with the Belle and Eagle Steamers, The General Steam Navigation Company operated tourist ships, including the MV *Royal Daffodil*, which was built in 1939 and saw service in the Second World War, rescuing at Dunkirk some 9,500 men in seven trips before being hit by a bomb. The quick thinking of her captain saw the soldiers go to the port side, which lifted the starboard side out of the water enough that it could be patched. She had light entertainment on board in the 1960s, including Gene Vincent in 1962, but was scrapped in 1967. She is shown here in June 1961 opposite Butler's Wharf.

Paddle pleasure steamers were in terminal decline by the late 1950s and had all but disappeared from Britain's rivers and estuaries. The Red Funnel steamer *Princess Elizabeth* had once sailed from Southampton and Southsea to the Isle of Wight and Bournemouth but was sold by 1959 and eventually became a floating restaurant on the Thames. She's shown here on 23 August 1975, and having survived the evacuation of Dunkirk, it is fitting that she now resides in Dunkirk, with her engines and boilers removed, as a conference centre.

The motor tanker *Druid Stone* (236 tons, built 1967) passing the Royal Festival Hall on 10 August 1971. The Hall was built for the 1951 Festival of Britain and is now a world-class theatre and part of the South Bank complex. *Druid Stone* belonged to Cory Tank Craft Ltd.

The 282-ton Dutch motor vessel *Holland* (1962), passing the Palace of Westminster on 5 August 1974.

The *Royalty* (79 tons, built 1913) and *Queen Elizabeth* (93 tons, built 1924) on 20 July 1960. Both vessels were built for J. Mears by Salters at Oxford. Despite a radical overhaul with enclosed lounges and a built in bridge, *Royalty* is still recognizable as the ship shown here. In 1940, she rescued many sick and injured from the beaches of Dunkirk. *Queen Elizabeth* was sold to Thames Launches in 1947 and by 2006 was operated by Colliers Launches. Another Mears ship built by Salters was the *Marchioness*, which was sunk with the loss of 53 lives in 1989.

The Singapore-registered MV *Sea Maas* (499 tons, built 1974) at Hungerford Bridge on 4 November 1978.

The West German MV *Maren C* (400 tons, built 1955) on 19 July 1975.

The many bridges of the River Thames resulted in a unique style of ship built to navigate the upper river. Here the *Fulham IV* (1,562 tons, built 1939) passes Cannon Street Station on 21 May 1950.

The Port of London Authority's steam yacht *St Katharine* (337 tons, built 1927) in the Pool of London on 8 July 1958.

Outside Hay's Wharf is the Dutch MV *Jean-E* (455 tones, built 1951) on 22 October 1961. Next door is Chamberlain's Wharf, built *c.* 1862, and taken over by Hay's Wharf in 1925 but by 1969 had been closed. Nearby is Hay's Galleria, utilising warehouses for shopping in what was once London's larder.

The cable ship *Cable Enterprise* (4,358grt, built 1964) in the Pool of London on 4 August 1964. Dressed overall in flags, she is on her maiden arrival in London.

The ill-fated paddle steamer *Queen of the South* was originally a Clyde paddle steamer called the *Jeanie Deans*. Bought to operate pleasure trips from the Pool of London, she was not a success and after two seasons (1966 and 1967), the *Queen of the South* was scrapped in December 1967. *Queen of the South* is shown here on 9 June 1967.

First mentioned in the 1590s as a place for landing grain, Irongate Wharf was destroyed by fire in 1846. The General Steam Navigation Co. had its wharves at Irongate. The Dutch vessel MV *Tycha* (499 tons, built 1962) is shown here on 13 July 1962.

At the Carron & Continental Wharves on 27 August 1961, the German steamer *Portia* (999 tons, built 1911) unloads.

The Carron & Continental Wharves at Wapping with the Norwegian MV *Jo-Frey* (498 tons, built 1955) on 13 July 1966. The Carron Company made its fortune building carronades and cannon for the Royal Navy, and operated its own shipping line from Scotland to London, using the port of Grangemouth. Latterly making post office pillarboxes and telephone boxes, the company went bust during the 1980s recession.

The Dutch freighter MV *Mitropa* (499 tons, built 1956) at the Carron & Continental Wharves on 29 June 1968.

The Danish training ship *Danmark* (790 tons, built 1933) on 19 May 1968. Used by the Danish merchant marine as a training ship, she was in America for the New York World's Fair and remained in the US for the duration of the war. *Danmark* was used to train some 5,000 US Cadets before returning home in 1945. She still survives and is a common sight in the Tall Ships Races. She is well known in the UK as she was one of seven vessels used during the filming of *The Onedin Line*.

Even today, the Pool of London sees many visiting motor yachts. On 26 May 1968, the *Shemara* (878 tons, built 1938) was visiting. She was owned by Lord and Lady Docker and many parties were held on board. By 1968 she was owned by Harry Hyman, a property tycoon. She has been fully restored at a cost of millions of pounds.

The South Eastern Gas Board's *Kingston* (1,873 tones, built 1956) in the lower Pool on 7 September 1968. Much of Britain's gas was once provided by coal gas and these colliers spent their entire careers transporting coal from the north of England to London, where it would be converted to coke and coal gas. The many power stations along the Thames helped cause the smogs of the 1950s.

The *Princess Elizabeth* on 1 August 1971. She was built in Southampton for Red Funnel.

The German charitable ship MV *Logos* was built in 1949 and met her end on a reef off Chile in 1987. She is shown here in London on 20 February 1971.

HMS *Plymouth* visits London on 3 July 1971. She was a Rothesay-class frigate, launched in 1959, which saw in the Cod Wars off Iceland as well as in the Falklands War. Decommissioned in 1988, she was preserved at Glasgow and Birkenhead until 2012 when she was sold for scrap.

Trinity House operates the lighthouses of England. To serve many of the outlying buoys, lightships and lighthouses, Trinity House operated a fleet of ships, including the *Patricia* (1,073grt, built 1938), shown here on 16 October 1971.

The Townsend Thoresen ferry *Free Enterprise II* berthed as the *Evening News* Motor Racing Showboat on 4 January 1972. She was built in 1965 in the Netherlands and scrapped in Alang, India, in 2003.

The brand new Danish DFDS ferry *Dana Regina* is passed by the *Maren C* on 4 July 1974. *Dana Regina*'s maiden voyage was on 8 July 1974 from Harwich to Esbjerg and she was sold in 1990. She has ended up with Latvian owners and is still in

Left: Another maiden arrival to the Pool of London was the Blue Star Line's MV *Andalucia Star* (9,784grt), shown here passing through Tower Bridge on 11 July 1975. Chartered to the Government in 1983 for transport duties to the Falklands, she was sold for scrapping in 2010.

Below: Perhaps the best photographed of London's wharves was the New Fresh Wharf. The photographs invariably taken from London bridge show a changing scene, as the wharf itself was expanded and skyscrapers were constructed behind it. In 1951, the Swedish Lloyd steamer *Patricia* (7,700grt) entered service and is shown here on 25 May that year.

New Fresh Wharf was under construction during 1939, when war started, and was not completed until after the war. The wharf could handle ships of up to 10,000 tons and many ships transporting fruit and general cargo called here. Vessels of the Aznar Line of Spain were frequent visitors. Here is the *Monte Buitre* (1,808grt, built 1929) on 27 April 1954, with scaffolding where the extensions of New Fresh Wharf will be.

Cargo is being discharged into lighters from the Belgian MV *Santiago* (1,290grt, built 1954) on 19 July 1954. Construction work of the extensions to the wharf are taking place and the façade is already in place.

The Aznar Line's *Monte Umbe* (9,971grt, built 1959) at New Fresh Wharf on 31 August 1961.

Above left: Cunard's MV *Phrygia* (3,534grt, built 1955) at New Fresh Wharf on 6 September 1963. Built in Port Glasgow, she was used on Cunard's Mediterranean cargo service, *Phrygia* was sold in September 1965 and renamed *Dimitris N.*

Above right: The 1949 Yugoslavian motor vessel *Plod* at New Fresh Wharf on 23 June 1965.

The MV *Kimolos* (4,866grt, built 1939) was a Greek cargo vessel and is shown here on 21 August 1967.

Berthed at New Fresh Wharf on 27 June 1967 is the brand new MV *Dragon*, which sailed from Southampton for P&O Normandy Ferries to France (and initially to Spain) until sold to Townsend Thoresen in 1985 and transferred to the Le Havre route.

Blue Star's MV *Canadian Star* (6,274grt, built 1957) photographed from under London Bridge on 28 September 1967.

Wilson Line's MV *Rollo* (2,499grt, built 1954) was an infrequent visitor to the Thames. With a skyscraper being built behind, New Fresh Wharf would succumb to the developers and in 1977 was replaced by an office block. Adelaide House to the left still survives. This view dates to 12 November 1967.

Many of the warehouses at St Katharine Dock were knocked down in the mid-1970s and the contrast between this and the next scene is obvious. New building is already taking place behind the tug *Challenge* (212 tons, built 1931) on 5 July 1974.

Next to The Tower of London and London Bridge is the only major project in London by Thomas Telford, St Katharine Dock. Work started in 1827 with some 11,500 people losing their homes as the work commenced. The dock was too small for the ships that would soon be in service and was never truly commercially successful. Bombing during the Second World War effectively sealed the fate of the docks and they were the first London docks to close, in 1968, although small vessels still used the dock into the 1970s. Here, the MV *Dannebrog* (93 tons, built 1901) lies in St Katharine Dock on 24 February 1974.

The auxiliary sailing barge *Lady Daphne* (117 tons, built 1923), of Rochester, turns in St Katharine Dock on 4 November 1976. The dock now has a modern yacht marina and housing, with some office development.

At Tower Stairs Tier you can find the only deep river solo mooring in Central London. Nowadays, you can berth close to HMS *Belfast*, and among superyachts, as well as the occasional passenger ship, such as Residensea's *The World*. On 10 June 1954, however, you would have been berthed next to the Dutch cargo vessel MV *Grebbestroom* (748 tons, built 1946).

General Steam Navigation Co.'s MV Queen of the Channel (1,472grt, built 1949) was a replacement for a ship of the same name sunk at Dunkirk. She is shown here off Tower Pier on 23 July 1954.

The steam yacht *St Katharine* (351grt, built 1927) was built in Dartmouth at a cost of £21,512 for the Port of London Authority as a survey yacht. She was the first vessel in the Port of London to engage the enemy when, in November 1939, her gunners fought off German aircraft. She was used as a floating restaurant until 2008, when she was rebuilt as *The Yacht London*. She is shown here at Tower Pier on 14 June 1965.

Built in 1924, the MV *Ferry Belle* was constructed for the Gosport & Portsea Waterman's Steam Launch Company and spent the years till 1966 in Portsmouth harbour. Sold to Coakley's Launches, she ran between Westminster, Tower Pier and Greenwich and is shown here in Coakley service on 8 July 1968 at Tower Bridge Pier.

MacBraynes' MV *Clansman* at Tower Pier on 9 January 1969. Built in 1964, she is rather far away from her home patch of the Western Isles.

The MV *Queen of the Isles* leaving Tower Pier on 24 May 1969. Built for the Isles of Scilly Steamship Co. in Bristol in 1964, she was chartered onto the Thames numerous times between 1966 and 1970. She was sold to Tonga as the *Olohava* and sailed there until 1982. In 2001, she ran aground in the Solomon Islands and remains there today.

The *Queen of the Isles*, Tower Pier, 21 June 1969.

Right: The Thames spritsail barge *May* (59 tons, built 1891) at Tower Pier on 8 October 1971.

Below: The Spanish MV *Sierra Lucena* (1,592grt, built 1967) at Chambers Wharf, Bermondsey, on 18 June 1971.

Aground at low tide at Chambers Wharf is another Spanish vessel, the MV *Guayadeque* (1,189grt, built 1965). Nowadays, the site of Chambers Wharf is the preferred location for a huge sewage tunnel.

The Dutch MV *Poolster* (1,187grt, built 1962) at low tide on 10 October 1971 at Chambers Wharf.

On the north bank of the river at Limehouse is the Regent's Canal Dock, built in 1820, was designed for transshipment between ocean going vessels and canal barges heading to and from the Midlands. After a period of decline, the dock has seen much construction of housing. On 13 November 1978, the *Artemis K*, a Panamanian-registered ferry was berthed in the dock.

The Norwegian fishing boat *Sortral* (118 tons, built 1938) berthed at Billingsgate jetty on 30 May 1949. A conveyer is ready to unload the vessel directly into Billingsgate market.

Outside their base at St John Wharf is W.H.J. Alexander's *Sun XIX* on 31 August 1961. *Sun XIX* was barely five years old.

On 19 September 1952, the *Crested Eagle* is laid up, her upperworks covered in canvas, with the General Steam Navigation Co.'s cargo vessel *Woodcock* astern at the company's wharf.

At St John's Wharf, the *Sun XX* looks rather the worse for wear, despite being only eight years old on 29 October 1965.

The 1920 sailing vessel *Cray* at W. H. J. Alexander's on 9 May 1971.

Chapter 2

Surrey Commercial Dock

The Norwegian heavy-lift ship *Belevelyn* (4,696grt, built 1946) in the Surrey Commercial Dock on 20 September 1953. The Surrey Commercial Docks were a series of docks in operation from 1696 to 1969, although ships were still using parts into 1970. The docks themselves were simply unable to cope with containerisation and the growth in cargo ship size.

Cunard's 7,301grt SS *Andria* in the Surrey Commercial Docks on 25 August 1957. The docks were heavily damaged during the Blitz but the South Dock saw use for construction of the Mulberry harbours that were successfully used after D-Day.

Denmark's MV *Nordpol* (4,919grt, built 1955) in Greenland Dock, 5 October 1957. Over 90 per cent of the water area of the Surrey Docks has been filled in and Greenland Dock is one of the few remaining areas of water in Rotherhithe and now includes a watersports centre.

Built in 1944, the SS *St Helena* is shown here in the Greenland Dock on 24 June 1959.

Lamport & Holt Line's MV *Rubens* in Greenland Dock, 24 May 1960. Built in Sunderland in 1952, she was scrapped in Pakistan in 1978. The Greenland Dock got its name from the many whaling ships that used the dock from the seventeenth century onwards. It was originally known as Howland's Wet Dock and had accommodation for over 120 sailing ships.

The tug *Sunrise* tows the MV *Baltic Express* in the Canada Dock on 16 March 1961. By the nineteenth century, almost 85 per cent of the land area of the peninsula was part of the dock system here, which comprised nine docks, six timber ponds and a canal.

The Bank Line's MV *Foylebank* (5,671grt, built 1955) in Greenland Dock on 16 March 1961.

MV *Beaverbank* (5,690grt, built 1953) on 27 February 1962. By the mid-1960s the growth in containerization was leading to the decline of the Surrey Docks system.

Canada Dock on 25 September 1963, with construction of tower blocks in the background. The ships in dock include, from left to right, the Greek MV *Cypros*, the Russian MV *Alatyrles*, the Brazilian *Loide-Venezuela* and the British *Mary K*.

On charter to Cunard Lake Services is the German MV *Lobivia* (4,072grt, built 1958) in Surrey Commercial Docks on 2 October 1963.

Surrounded by lighters is the Russian MV *Gulbene* (3,743grt, built 1964) in Surrey Commercial Dock on 28 October 1966.

On 28 March 1967, the American Lykes Lines' SS *Leslie Lykes* (9,891grt, built 1962) could be found in the Surrey Commercial Docks system. A docker has a cup of tea on the lighter in the foreground.

It is 26 September 1967 and the Surrey Commercial Docks still look as if they will continue forever. The Greek steamer *Hermes Leader* (2,872grt, built 1944) unloads timber.

With black smoke belching from her funnel, the Russian steamship *Kolpino* (3,247grt, built 1958) is shown leaving the Surrey Commercial Docks on 22 November 1967. The tower blocks shown being constructed on p. 36 (bottom) are completed

On 22 November 1967, the tug *Sun III* hauls the Russian steamer *Banga* from the quayside, as she prepares to return to the Baltic. The Russian ship is barely a year old.

With three of her crew visible, the MV *Roan* and a lighter were in the Surrey Commercial Dock on 5 December 1967. At one point, every quay would have been full of ships, with stevedores working overtime to discharge vessels here. By 1967, the dock had three ships.

The Rumanian MV *Mamaia* (3,969grt, built 1930) on 5 December 1967.

Cargoes of timber can be seen on the lighters in front of the Rumanian MV *Baia Mare* (3,090grt, built 1965) in the Surrey dock system.

The coaster MV *Petrel* (496grt, built 1965) on 1 March 1970 in the Surrey Commercial Docks system.

New Zealand Shipping Co.'s MV *Piako* (9,986grt, built 1962) in the Surrey Commercial Docks on 7 March 1970. Built by Alexander Stephen, at Linthouse, Glasgow, she was the last ship built for NZSC in their yellow funnel colour.

The Danish MV *Ajfos* (300grt, built 1969) on 15 March 1970.

1970 was to see the closure of the Surrey Commercial Docks and in the last few scenes, there are few ships in view, unlike in the 1950s and 60s when each quay had a ship berthed at it. The German MV *Otto* (300grt, built 1950) is berthed next to warehouses once used to house grain and valuable timbers from all over the world.

Porters at the Surrey Commercial Docks were known as deal porters after the baulks of deal (timber) they carried on their shoulders. The Surrey Commerical Docks perhaps accounted for 80 per cent of all the timber imported into London. Here the *Santa Katerina II* of Greece unloads into lighters on 30 March 1970.

Despite the decline, some parts of the Surrey Docks system looked busy in 1970. On 30 March, the vessels in the Greenland Dock included the MV *Courland*, MV *Beechbank* and the *Machaon*.

Unloading timber on 1 July 1970 is the Russian steamer SS *Uralmash* (3,080grt, built 1936). By 1981, the Surrey Commercial Docks were no more! Now some 5,500 homes cover the peninsula and there is little area in water. Surrey Quays shopping centre opened in 1988 and the area has proven to be a popular place to live today.

Chapter 3

West India Dock system

Once a common sight in London's docklands, a lone whaler visits Millwall Dock on 9 October 1949. The *William Scoresby* was built in 1926, when whaling was at its peak. Large whale factory ships in the Antarctic were catching some 1,000 whales a year in the short summer season in the Ross Sea.

Just sold and being renamed from *Villegas* to *Aghios Lazaros*, this Cypriot ship is shown here on 30 June 1970 in India & MIllwall Docks. Soon she would sail from London for her new Mediterranean owners.

Cunard's *Parthia* (5,149grt) was built in 1963 and is shown here on 7 July 1970.

The tug *Lord Ritchie* (109 tons, built 1959) tows the Russian freighter MV *Nordvik* (4,846grt, built 1965) into her berth in the India & Millwall Docks on 25 August 1970.

Cable ships play an important function, even today, laying and repairing subsea cables which are still vital for telecommunications. The first transatlantic cable was made in London and in two attempts in the 1850s and 1860s a cable was laid between the United Kingdom and Newfoundland, finally being completed by Brunel's *Great Eastern*. Here the steamer *Cable Monarch* of 1946 is shown in the India & Millwall Docks on 26 September 1970.

The Cypriot-registered MV *Anenome* (7,168grt, built 1952) surrounded by lighters on 1 November 1970.

Many of the Ben Line vessels never ever visited their home port of Leith as it was too small to accommodate the larger Ben liners. Here, the *BenMhor* (7,755grt, built 1949) is in the India & Millwall Dock system on 1 November 1970.

Harrison Line's MV *Factor* (6,533grt, built 1948) in the India & Millwall Docks on 6 December 1970.

Clan Robertson (7,955grt, built 1965) on 6 December 1970.

Right: Ellerman Line's MV *City of Lichfield* (7,012grt, built 1961) on 14 November 1971.

Below: The tug *Fossa* in the entrance to the India & Millwall Docks. Built in 1961, she was shown here ten years later on 18 December 1971. Tugs were the lifeblood of the dock system, and without them the docks could never have functioned.

The West German MV *Suncapri* (9,402grt, built 1969) has just been towed into the entrance dock by the tug *Fossa* on 18 December 1971.

On 30 January 1972, the India & Millwall Docks were home to the West German motor vessels *Aquila* (5,862grt, built 1959) and the *Astrid* (3,198grt, built 1952) as well as Harrison Line's MV *Factor*.

The MV *Salerno* (1,559grt, built 1965) and the two-year-old German MV *Nordstrand* (4,794grt) in the India & Millwall Docks on 30 January 1972.

On her maiden arrival to the India & Millwall Docks is the brand-new Finnish ferry MV *Aallotar* (7,801grt), photographed in the entrance dock on 20 February 1972. She is dressed overall in flags.

Above: The coaster MV *Blackstakes* of Rochester on 20 February 1972.

Left: The Strick Line operated many ships in the 1950s and 60s. The MV *Turkistan* (9,270grt, built 1963) is shown here on 20 February 1972.

With a backdrop of huge silos, the Dutch coaster MV *Mangen* (1,534grt, built 1969) in the India & Millwall Docks on 20 February 1972.

MV *Embassage* (1,428grt, built 1968), registered in Newcastle, in the India & Millwall Docks on 19 March 1972.

The Thames sailing barge *Raybel* was built in 1920 by Wills & Packham in Sittingbourne, Kent. Shown here on 15 April 1972, she is built mainly of wood but with steel keel and iron beams. She was fitted with a Kelvin diesel engine in 1939 and used by the military on the Clyde during the war. In 1977, after a year long restoration, she returned to the water with her mast restored and can now be hired out.

The Greek cargo ship MV *Santa Maja* (9,100grt, built 1972) makes one of her first calls into the India & Millwall Docks on 15 April 1972.

Another Greek ship, the MV *Tara* (4,010grt, built 1961) on 21 October 1972.

Two views of British India Steam Navigation Co.'s SS *Nardana* (8,511grt, built 1956) entering the docks on 21 October 1972. Owned by P&O, BI was one of the largest shipping companies in Britain, but many of their ships never sailed here as they operated in the Pacific and Indian Ocean and to the east coast of Africa.

MV *Morvada* (11,143grt, built 1971) is barely a year old when she visited India & Millwall Docks on 12 November 1972.

Owned by the London & Rochester Trading Co., the MV *Rohoy* (172grt, built 1966) is shown on 12 November 1972. She was built in Frindsbury, opposite Chatham. Shipbuilding had taken place there since at least 1745 and over 100 Thames barges were built here.

The Danish coaster MV *Bent Barsøe* (499grt, built 1970) on 10 February 1973.

Aznar Lines' MV *Monte Arucas* (4,691grt, built 1956) on 10 February 1973. As seen earlier, many Aznar ships called at New Fresh Wharf in the Pool but their ships also used the India & Millwall Docks.

Owned by E. A. Horlock and R. Sully, the Thames sailing barge *Phoenician* was built in 1922 by Wills & Packham. She was converted to a motor barge in 1949, as shown here, and is shown here on her last year of commercial service on 25 February 1973. That year she was sold out of trade to an Albert Groom, who used her for chartering and was based in Ipswich. She spent some time in the West India Docks after this and following her restoration at Pin Mill, she is now based in St Katharine Docks.

At one time, it was possible to enter the docks and wander round viewing the ships. Here, a man and his daughter watch the MV *Bruno*, a Norwegian ship of 2,752grt, leaving the India & Millwall Docks on 1 April 1973.

Spanish sailors touch up the white hull of the Aznar Line's MV *Monte Arucas* on 8 April 1973. The threat of containerization was real and the dock system could not cope with the changes in shipping in the 1970s. Containerisation meant that ships could be unloaded quickly and easily using little man-power, while goods could easily be transported via truck or railway to their onward destination and it was merely a matter of time before the loss of thousands of jobs in the docks and their ultimate closure.

Furness Prince Line's MV *Mendip Prince* (1,459grt, built 1970) on 8 April 1973.

Riding high in the water, the Harrison Line's MV *Statesman* (6,162grt, built 1964) has been emptied of cargo on 15 April 1973. All of the Harrison Line ships were named after occupations and the most famous was the SS *Politician*, of *Whisky Galore* fame. Lost off Eriskay with 28,000 bottles of whisky aboard, the locals salvaged much. A recent sale of two bottles recovered from the *Politician* saw them fetch £12,000.

The Safmarine *S.A. Merchant* (9,517grt, built 1955) on 5 May 1973. The South Africans founded Safmarine in 1946, using three Victory-class, American-built ships, with their first new ships appearing in the 1950s. *S.A. Merchant* was one of those, built on the Clyde, and with a top speed of 17kt, she carried general cargo, principally between South Africa and London.

The 1951 tug *Plagal* tows the Greek MV *Corinthic* (10,914grt, built 1959) into the India & Millwall Docks on 30 June 1973. The tug *Plagal* was built in Hessle, East Yorkshire, and scrapped in Barking in 1986. She was part of the Port of London Authority's fleet of tugs.

Chapter 4

Woolwich, North Woolwich & Greenwich

Awaiting custom at North Woolwich pier on 8 September 1960 are the tugs *Java* (128 tons, built 1905) and *Racia* (163 tons, built 1930).

Woolwich has had a ferry since the fourteenth century and with increased traffic, a vehicular ferry has existed there for many years. In 1963, it was all change and new ferries, built in Dundee, came into service. On 27 May 1963, *John Burns* had just entered service.

The three new vessels replaced four paddle steamers, one of which, *Gordon* (625 tons), is shown here high and dry for maintenance on 27 May 1963.

One of the many coasters that plied the river, the MV *Harry Richardson* (1,777 tons, built 1950) was designed specifically with low superstructure so that it could pass under the many bridges beyond the Pool of London. She is shown here on 3 July 1972 at Hanover Hole Tier.

Many ferries have operated on the Thames, carrying passengers to Scandinavia, France, Belgium and the Netherlands. A new entrant, and certainly one of the fastest, was the Boeing jetfoil *Flying Princess*, shown here off Woolwich on 4 June 1977. Operated by P&O Ferries on the St Katharine Dock–Zeebrugge route, the jetfoil could reach speeds of 40 knots and more.

With a Woolwich ferry in the background, the tug *Charlock* (42 tons, built 1962) is shown off Woolwich on 21 September 1982. *Charlock* was built in Dartford for the Charrington Lighterage Co. and was eventually sold to Canvey Island as *Charloc*.

At Wm Cory's wharf is the Danish-refrigerated vessel MV *Freezer Scan* (1,243grt, built 1968) on 3 July 1971.

In Deptford Creek at low tide on 3 August 1980 is the Spanish MV *Urraki* (750grt, built 1975). She is probably unloading ether coal for the power station or building materials for some of the many developments beginning to take place along the river.

The *Eileen M* (1,018grt, built 1966) in Deptford Creek, with Deptford West power station in the background on 13 July 1981. There had been a power station here since the 1880s and the one shown here was constructed on a dry dock in 1929. It closed in 1983 and was demolished in 1992, with housing now covering the site, although the jetty still remains.

Barely a week later, on 18 July 1981, the Spanish MV *Jose Esquivel* and the British MV *Birkenhead Miller* unload at Deptford.

The MV *Cirrus*, a Swedish motor ship of 7,877grt, at Greenwich Tier on 16 March 1961.

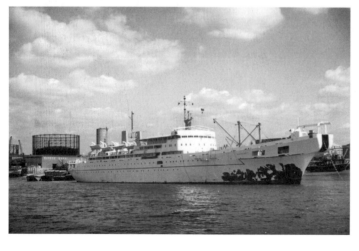

Cable & Wireless's cable ship *Mercury* (8,962grt, built 1962) opposite Morden Wharf on 29 August 1964. Despite an age of only two years, she is rather weather-worn. Ever since the construction of the Atlantic Telegraph in 1858-1865, London had been a major producer of submarine cables and the *Mercury* was the modern equivalent of the Thames-built *Great Eastern*, which successfully laid the first transatlantic telegraph cable.

The Spanish ocean liner MV *Cabo San Vicente* at Greenwich on a rare visit to London on 19 July 1967. Built in 1959 in Spain, she was used on the Europe-South America route and started cruising in the early 1970s with the decline of the passenger trade.

Passing Greenwich on 19 July 1967 is the Norwegian MV *Baldrian* (1,419grt, built 1947).

Eastern Princess on 26 September 1970 at Greenwich. Built in 1942, the *Eastern Princess* was an ex-Fairmile motor launch ordinarily sailing out of Great Yarmouth on pleasure cruises.

Swanage Queen at Greenwich on 9 May 1971. Built in 1948, she was seen in and around Swanage Bay, giving pleasure trips to sun-seeking holidaymakers. From 1971, she was on the Thames, owned by Meridian Line. She is currently a houseboat in Hoo Marina.

Cruising into Greenwich on 3 July 1971 was the Ybarra Line's MV *Cabo San Vicente*. She is dressed overall in flags. Many ships came as far as Greenwich for London as the journey up or down to the Pool could only be made one way in larger vessels. The Pilot's job was tricky, manouevering a 15,000-ton vessel up the Thames backwards for many miles.

The Argentinian cruiser *La Argentina* off Greenwich on 9 October 1971. Naval vessels from all over the world still make visits to London.

On 31 October 1976,
the tug *Arthur Darling*
(50 tons, built 1946)
and the motor boat
Pointer are berthed at
Greenwich.

The *Cornelia Bosma*
(1,369grt, built 1971) is
getting a name change
to *Atlantic Comet* on
23 August 1978, at
Greenwich.

The MV *Astor*, a
German-owned liner,
visits Greenwich on 17
July 1985. There are
still many lighters in
evidence on this part
of the river. Sold to
Safmarine, she ship was
purchased by Saga to
become *Saga Pearl II*
and is now *Quest for
Adventure* for the Saga
Group's Adventure
Cruises subsidiary.

Chapter 5

The Royal Docks

The 1950-built Argentinian steamer *Uruguay* in Royal Victoria Dock on 16 March 1967.

On 30 March 1967, this panoramic view of the Royal Victoria Dock has the Blue Star Line's *Wellington Star* (12,539grt, built 1952) in dock, as well as another Blue Star vessel. *Wellington Star* was built by John Brown's and ended her career at a Taiwanese shipbreakers in 1979 after three years as a livestock carrier.

The Houlder Brothers' refrigerated SS *Hardwicke Grange* (10,388grt, built 1961) at the Royal Victoria Dock on 30 March 1967. Hardwicke Grange was built by Hawthorn Leslie at Newcastle.

Royal Mail Lines' *Aragon* was one of a trio of vessels, built between 1959 and 1960, the other pair being *Amazon* and *Arlanza*. In 1965, the company was bought by Furness Withy and *Aragon* was transferred to Shaw Savill in 1969, becoming *Aranda*, before being sold in 1971 for conversion to a car transporter. She is shown here on 9 April 1967.

Hardwicke Grange in Royal Victoria Dock on 23 March 1967.

Royal Mail Lines' MV *Eden* (7,562grt, built 1956) was built by Harland & Wolff and was sold out of service after thirteen years to Neptune Orient Line, Singapore, and renamed *Neptune Garnet*.

Shaw Savill Line's MV *Delphic* (10,690grt, built 1949) was used on the New Zealand route and carried refrigerated and frozen meat. Here in the Royal Victoria Dock on 4 April 1969, she was scrapped in 1971. Shaw Savill at one point operated a joint service with White Star Line and the original *Delphic* was a White Star vessel on the joint service to New Zealand and Australia.

Adelaide Star was built in 1950 at John Brown's in Clydebank and scrapped in 1975 in South Korea after uneconomical damage to her engines. Shown here in Royal Victoria Dock on 4 April 1969, she was one of a set of four ships, two built at Clydebank and two at Cammell Laird's in Birkenhead. Her sister, *Auckland Star*, spent some eight years on the stocks due to steel and manpower shortages, not appearing until 1958.

Already some twenty years old, the SS *Duquesa* on 4 June 1969. She had originally been a Houlder ship and was transferred to Royal Mail Lines in 1968. In 1970, she was scrapped.

Another transfer to Royal Mail Lines from Houlder Bros was the MV *Duoro* (10,783grt, built 1946). Built as *Hornby Grange*, she was transferred in 1969, not long before she is shown here on 9 November of that year. She was scrapped in 1972.

Although famous for their series of liners built for the Southampton-Cape route Union-Castle Line also operated from London on the East African service. The MV *Richmond Castle* was built in 1944 as a refrigerated cargo ship and is shown here on 28 February 1970.

With *Duoro* astern, the two coasters *Roina* (172 tons, built 1966) and *Josh Francis* (137 tons, built 1954) are in the Royal Victoria Dock on 17 October 1970.

17 October 1970 and the German motor vessel *Bellavia* (5,514grt, built 1959) is berthed in the Royal Victoria Dock.

Another long-established line using the Port of London was the Port Line, here, MV *Port Sydney* (11,683grt, built 1955) is shown on 17 October 1970. Sold three years later to the Carras Group, Greece, she was renamed *Akrotiri Express*.

Constructed in 1966, the 10.300grt MV *Orcoma* was built for the Pacific Steam Navigation Co. Shown here on 17 October 1970, she was sold to Indonesia in 1979 and renamed *Ek Daya Samudera*.

Blue Funnel was more well known in Liverpool and Birkenhead than in London, but this view of 13 February 1971 shows the SS *Talthybius* (7,313grt, built 1944) in the Royal Victoria Dock. *Talthybius* was ex-*Salina Victory*, and was purchased from US Maritime Commission, renamed *Polydorus*, operated by NSOM, and in 1960 transferred to Blue Funnel, renamed *Talthybius* (3). She was scrapped in 1971.

Built in 1950 as *Bellerophon* (3) for the Blue Funnel Line, this vessel was transferred in 1957 to Glen Line and renamed *Cardiganshire*. Shown in the Royal Victoria Dock on 17 April 1971, she was transferred the following year back to Blue Funnel as *Bellerophon*.

The Norwegian MV *Sol Laila* (5,150grt, built 1952) in the Royal Docks system on 17 October 1971.

Berthed at the Co-operative Wholesale Society's berth in the Royal Victoria Dock on 17 October 1971 is the *Port Pirie* (10,537grt, built 1947) of Port Line. Laid up here prior to disposal, within a few months *Port Pirie* had gone to the breakers' yard.

Owned by Elder Dempster and built in Grangemouth in 1967, the MV *Carway* was one of the first bespoke car carriers, with a capacity of about 400 family cars. It was used by both Ford and the Rootes Group to transport new vehicles to Scandinavia. With five decks, and a ventilation system that ensured fresh air during car loading and unloading, the *Carway* was a huge success and the first of many vessels that now can carry thousands of cars at one time. She is berthed in the Royal Victoria Dock on 18 March 1973.

Blue Star Line's *Montevideo Star* (8,257grt, built 1956) on 11 August 1973. Built as *Newcastle Star*, she was renamed in 1973 and sold in 1976 to Cyprus, and renamed *Golden Madonna*.

The Argentinian SS *Libertad* (12,563grt, built 1950) entering the Royal Dock system on 15 July 1967.

MV *Industria* (7,744grt, built 1960) of Hartlepool was originally built as *Silverisle* for Silver Line before being renamed as *Industria* for Metcalfe Shipping in 1965. She was broken up at Gadani Beach, Pakistan, in April 1984.

The New Zealand Shipping Co.'s MV *Mataura* in the Royal Albert Dock on 20 April 1969. Built in 1968, she was transferred to Federal Steam Navigation Co. in 1971, then onto P&O. She ended her life with Greek owners as *Macedonian Reefer*.

Built for Ropner as the *Swiftpool* in 1954, *Chalka* (6,565grt) was purchased by the British India Steam Navigation Co. and renamed. In 1972, she was sold to Singapore and renamed *Golden Bear*.

The 1925 tug *Sun XV* is in position to haul the Liberian-registered MV *San Nicolaos* (8,952grt, built 1957) away from her berth in the Royal Albert Dock on 9 May 1969.

Shaw Savill's *Gothic* was made famous when she was new and was used by HM the Queen as a Royal Yacht before *Britannia* was completed. Painted white for the occasion, she visited Australia and New Zealand. Here in the Royal Albert Dock on 9 May 1969, she sailed for Taiwan soon after for breaking. Despite looking spick and span, she had become redundant due to the jet airliner and was scrapped despite many years of life left in her.

Above: The Romanian MV *Galati* (3,161grt, built 1960) and the New Zealand Shipping Co.'s *Pipiriki.* The steamer *Pipiriki* (7,195grt, built 1944) had perhaps a year of life left in her before being scrapped, when she was photographed on 17 October 1970 in the Royal Albert Dock. She ended her life with the Federal Steam Navigation Co. in 1971.

Left: The dock system also had many dry docks for repair and overhaul of ships. Here, the Norwegian MV *Northland* (4,908grt, built 1962) is dry-docked on 1 November 1970 in the Royal Albert Dock.

Ellerman Line's MV *City of Worcester* (6,978grt, built 1960) in the Royal Albert Dock on 15 November 1970. After nineteen years service, *City of Worcester* was sold to Greek shipowners and renamed *Maria Diamanto*.

Built in 1947 to replace war losses, the British India Steam Navigation Co.'s MV *Purnea* (5,340grt) is berthed in the Royal Albert Dock on 15 November 1970. In 1971 she sailed for Spain and was scrapped. Many British India ships never returned to Britain as most of the company's routes were between India and Africa and around the Far East.

Brocklebank Line's MV *Mahout* (9,153grt, built 1963) in the Royal Albert Dock on 13 February 1971. She was sold in 1978, after fifteen years with Brocklebank, and renamed *Aglaos*.

The Alexander SS Co.'s MV *Tewkesbury* (8,532grt, built 1959) in the Royal Albert Dock on 1 February 1971.

Surrounded by a forest of propellers, the Shaw Savill *Canopic* is dry-docked in the Royal Albert Dock on 6 March 1971. In 1976, she was sold to Cyprus and renamed *Capetan Nicolas*. A propeller could take upwards of three months to cast and machine and spares were often made at the same time as the ones fitted to a ship and stored for future use. Stone's of Deptford was one of the premier makers of propellers in Britain, making blades for the *Queen Mary* and *Normandie*, as well as White Star's *Majestic*.

The MV *Tarpon Surf* (8,001grt, built 1956) and Ellerman's *City of York* in the Royal Albert Dock on 3 April 1971.

Ships needed fuel and in and around the dock system small tankers would bunker them while they were berthed, loading or unloading. Here, the *Shell Dispenser* (239 tons, built 1963) is tied up, while in the background are the MV *Bendearg* (8,199grt, built 1964) and the Singapore-registered MV *Neptune Zircon* (6,850grt, built 1961) in the Royal Albert Dock on 17 October 1971.

Ships of the Harrison Line were named after trades and professions, and the MV *Author* (8,715grt, built 1958) was no exception. Ships of the Clan Line were named after Scottish clans, and the *Clan Menzies* (7,315grt, built 1958) is berthed on the opposite side of the dock on 17 October 1971.

A floating crane unloads the MV *Neptune Amethyst* (5,630grt, built 1969), while Blue Star's MV *Montreal Star* (7,365grt, built 1963) and Port Line's *Port Nelson* (10,138grt, built 1951) are berthed on the opposite side of the Royal Albert Dock on 17 December 1961.

Built by William Denny of Dumbarton for the Caledonian Steam Packet Co.'s Clyde Coast services in 1934, the venerable paddle steamer *Caledonia* was withdrawn in 1969 and sold to Bass-Charrington for service as a floating restaurant on the Thames. She is shown here as *Old Caledonia* in the Royal Albert Dock on 15 April 1972 almost ready to be berthed at the Victoria Embankment. Damaged by fire in 1980, she was scrapped soon after at Milton Creek, Kent.

MV *Donegal* (6,270grt, built 1957) in the Royal Albert Dock on 11 November 1972.

Hain Line's MV *Trevaylor* (8,256grt, built 1959) on 21 January 1973.

The tugs *Plankton* and *Plangent* on 2 July 1973.

Built in 1953, the New Zealand Shipping Co.'s MV *Otaki* (10,934grt) is dry-docked at Silley Weir's dry dock in the Royal Albert Dock system on 22 July 1973.

Tractors await loading onto the Ellerman Line's *City of London* (9,793grt, built 1970) on 22 July 1973.

Clan Line's *Clan Matheson* and Ellerman's *City of Ripon* in the Royal Albert Dock on 9 February 1974.

The coaster *Maguda* (170 tons, built 1959) in the Royal Albert Dock on 21 March 1974.

The former sailing barge MV *Niagara* was built in 1898 and is shown here some seventy-six years later on 31 March 1974.

The French cargo ship MV *Pointe Allegre* is towed stern first by the tug *Plasma* in the Royal Albert Dock on 20 April 1974.

In dry dock on 20 April 1974 is the MV *Cambrook* (1,574grt, built 1967).

After the building of the Humber Bridge, the paddlesteamer *Wingfield Castle* (556grt, built 1934) was sold and ended up in London. Originally built for the London & North Eastern Railway, she has ended her career in preservation in the town of her birth, Hartlepool, where she is open to the public as a museum ship. She is shown here on 27 July 1974 in the Royal Albert Dock immediately after withdrawal.

The motorized sailing barge *Hydrogen* (124 tons, built 1906) has made it into preservation and is now owned by Topsail Charters of Maldon, Essex, and has been restored into a condition similar to that when she was built. Here, on 26 January 1975, she was still a working vessel, and id depicted here in the Royal Albert Dock.

P&O's *Comorin* in the King George V Dock on 27 February 1967. Built in 1951 as *Singapore*, her name was changed to *Comorin* (2) in 1964, to *Pando Cove* in 1968 and was scrapped in Spain in 1972.

On the left is Houlder Bros' *Royston Grange* (10,262grt, built 1959) and on the right with a deck cargo and being towed by the tug *Plasma* is a Dutch vessel, the MV *Wonosari* (7,583grt, built 1942) on 2 September 1967. The warehouses behind were demolished and this is now the site of London City Airport.

Immediately after being sold to Orient Overseas Line, the ex-*Ruahine* (17,581grt, built 1951) of New Zealand Shipping Co. in the KGV Dock on 4 September 1968. Her name had been changed to *Oriental Rio*.

Glen Line's MV *Glenearn* (8,888grt, built 1938) in the King George V Dock on 4 April 1969. She was scrapped a year later.

Behind *Glenearn* is the New Zealand Shipping Co.'s *Rangitoto* (21,809grt, built 1949). *Rangitoto* was also sold to Oriental Overseas Line in 1969.

MV *Glengyle* with *Rangitoto* opposite. *Glengyle* was the fifth ship to have the name and was built in 1939. During the Second World War she was requisitioned as as HMS *Glengyle* and returned to Glen Line in 1948. In 1970 she went to Blue Funnel as *Deucalion* (5) and was scrapped in 1971.

Shaw Savill's MV *Akaroa* (18,565grt, built 1959) on 20 April 1969. She had been a Royal Mail Line ship and was sold for conversion to a car carrier.

Port Auckland berthed alongside *Port Chalmers* in the King George V Dock on 9 May 1969.

Shaw Savill's MV *Cretic* (11,151grt, built 1955) with Blue Star Line's MV *Australia Star* (10,025grt, built 1965) behind in the King George V Dock on 9 May 1969.

The *Ena* of Ipswich with Glen Line's *Glenalmond* behind on 31 August 1969. *Ena* was built in 1906 and served at Dunkirk as one of the little ships.

The tug *Napia* (261 tons, built 1943) on 4 June 1970.

Entering the Thames from the King George V system is BP's tanker *British Vision* (11,190grt, built 1954) on 10 January 1971.

Viewed through the bottom of one of the dockside cranes is Port Line's *Port Chalmers* (16,283grt, built 1968) on 13 February 1971.

A blizzard is blowing as the German MV *Iberia* (10,066grt, built 1970) manoeuvres in the King George V Dock on 6 March 1971.

Shaw Savill's *Aranda* (18,575grt, built 1960) in the King George V dock on 6 March 1971. When sold for conversion to a car carrier, she was renamed *Hoegh Traveller*.

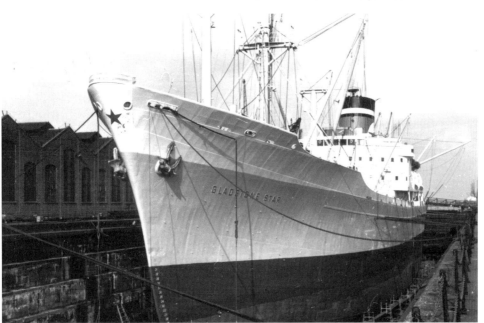

Blue Star's *Gladstone Star* is dry-docked in the repair yard at the King George V Dock on 23 May 1971.

The *Niagara* had a long career, having been built in 1898. Seventy-three years later, on 23 May 1971, she was still hard at work in the King George V Dock.

HMS *Belfast* was retired from Navy service in 1968, having served in both the Second World and Korean wars. She was refitted before becoming a museum ship in the Pool of London and is shown here in dry dock on 9 October 1971, receiving a new paint job before sailing up river.

Another view of *Belfast* in dry dock. Early in the Second World War she was extensively damaged by a magnetic mine in the Firth of Forth and was out of action for over two years.

The South African MV *Komatiland* (9,312grt, built 1956) in the KGV Dock on 9 October 1971.

The tug *Sun III* (150 tons, built 1966) awaits the call to help berth a ship on 9 October 1971.

Two coasters, the *Rohoy* of Rochester (172 tons, built 1966) and the *Cecil Gilders* (137grt, built 1957) of Colchster, in the King George V Dock on 28 November 1971.

The Royal Fleet Auxiliary *Tidesurge* (13,732grt, built 1956) in the King George V Drydock on 20 August 1972. This steam tanker would have sailed around the world replenishing Royal Navy warships on patrol. She was broken up in 1977 in Valencia, Spain.

Under repair in the King George V Drydock on 6 October 1974 is the Kuwaiti MV *Al Salehiah* (9,589grt, built 1973)

On the same day, the Pakistani MV *Bagh-E-Dacca* (8,967grt, built 1966) is under repair in one of the other dry docks.

A rare visitor to the King George V system on 19 January 1975 was the *Free Enterprise VII* (4,981grt, built 1973), a Townsend Thoresen cross-channel ferry.

The French Line's MV *Rochambeau* and the tug *Plankton* on 24 February 1977. On the left, in the distance is the Greek tanker *Panaghia A*.

Chapter 6

Tilbury, Gravesend & the Stage

The ferry *Tessa* (368grt, built 1924) at Tilbury landing Stage on 6 August 1960. A railway station was built by the London, Tilbury & Southend Railway in 1854 and ships were soon calling at a stage on the river.

The passenger ferry *Catherine* (259grt, built 1903) off Tilbury on 14 August 1960. The ferries sailed across the river between Tilbury and Southend, offering a service for workers. This was *Catherine*'s last year of service as she was replaced by a new vessel of the same name.

The newly-built *Catherine* off Tilbury on 12 August 1961. The ferries were operated by the railway company .

Right: P&O's *Arcadia* was built by John Brown at Clydebank and is shown here with the tug *Moorcock* at the Stage on 21 August 1963.

Below: Passing Tilbury on 26 August 1963 was the Nigerian MV *Nnamdi Azikiwe.*

This view gives an impression of just how busy the river could be, with the Italian liner *Flavia* berthing at the Stage, with P&O's *Himalaya* in mid-river on 26 June 1965.

As shore staff look on, the *Flavia* is tied up at the Stage.

Two young ship spotters look out onto the river as the tanker MV *Corstar* (3,379grt, built 1956) passes by the Stage on 26 June 1965.

P&O's *Himalaya* off Tilbury on 26 June 1965. *Himalaya* was built in 1949 but did not survive the early 1970s Suez oil crisis, which saw the price of fuel oil rise and which made older liners uneconomical. She was scrapped in 1974.

On an early visit to the Thames, the Norwegian America Line ship *Sagafjord* (24,002grt, built 1965) can be seen on the opposite side of the river on 6 May 1966. The Royal Mail Lines' *Aragon* is at the Stage.

The Londoner ferry sailing past the Stage on 18 June 1966. She was a Swedish ferry named *Princessan Christina*.

P&O's *Iberia* viewed from one of the river ferries as she berths at the Stage on 22 April 1967. The Ten Pound Pom emigration scheme to Australia was very much active then and ships were regularly sailing full of emigrants.

The ferry *Svea* (7,883grt, built 1966) sails down river on 8 July 1967.

The Polish liner *Batory* at the Stage on 30 August 1967. She had survived the war and had been used as a troopship.

British India Line used the *Uganda* for their East African service and latterly she was an educational cruise ship. She is well known for her stint in the Falklands as a hospital ship. Steam up, and creating a plume of black, sooty smoke, she is ready to leave the Stage on 4 May 1968.

The tug *Cervia* and the Dutch MV *Carebeka* on 21 September 1968.

The motor tanker *Baccarat* (293 tons, built 1959) passes the Stage on 19 July 1969.

The tug *Sun XXVII* and
the Polish liner *Stefan
Batory* at the Stage on 1
September 1969.

Having her name
painted at the Stage
is the German liner
Hamburg. She was built
in 1969 and is shown
here on 29 August
1973.

Russian liners were
frequent callers to the
Stage at Tilbury. Here,
on 5 September 1976,
is the MV *Mikhail
Kalinin* and the Greek
MV *Daphne*.

Sporting the corporate British Railways livery is the ferry *Catherine* on 12 July 1977. Sailing past the Stage is the barge *Gladys* of 1901 and the MV *Towerstream*.

The motor tanker *Buckingham* passes by the Stage on 2 November 1978, where the Russian MV *Kareliya* (16,631grt, built 1976) is berthed.

It is 14 April 1982 and the ships have changed. A container ship, the MV *Studland Bay* (16,482grt, built 1980) passes by the Russian MV *Odessa* (13,758grt, built 1974) at the Stage. Containerisation was to kill the docks closer to London but create opportunities at Tilbury itself, which saw an expansion as the upper docks closed down.

On 5 July 1965, the barges *Atrato* (95 tons, built 1898) and the sailing barge *Cambria* (79 tons, built 1906) were berthed in the Tilbury dock system.

The Dutch MV *Tero* (5,609grt, built 1949) on 5 July 1965 at Tilbury.

The Norwegian MV *Talabot* (6,104grt, built 1946) in Tilbury docks on 13 July 1966.

The Greek steamer *Eurybates* (6,373grt, built 1961) gets steam up in Tilbury Dock, 21 May 1969. With the tug *Ionia* at her stern and another at her bow, she is getting ready to depart.

The MV *Celtic Ferry* (5,556grt, built 1943) and the Port Line's *Port Victor* (10,390grt, built 1943) in Tilbury Dock on 21 May 1969.

The Pakistani MV *Bagh-E-Dacca* in Tilbury Dock on 19 July 1969.

With the Swedish Lloyd Ferry *Saga* behind her, the coaster *Peter Robin* is berthed at Tilbury on 26 October 1969.

Behind the *Peter Robin* were the two barges *Southdown* and *Cabby*.

British India Steam Navigation Co.'s MV *Chilka* (7,087grt, built 1950) in Tilbury on 26 October 1969.

In dry dock at Tilbury on 22 February 1970 is the BP tanker *British Resource* (11,200grt, built 1949).

The mainstay of the dock system were the small coasters, which could reach creeks and harbours the larger ships could not. Here, in Tilbury on 3 August 1974, are the MV *Bastion* (172 tons, built 1958) of Rochester and the *Moiler* (138 tons, built 1915).

Houlder Bros SS *Royston Grange* sails past Gravesend on 12 August 1961.

General Steam Navigation Co. operated pleasure steamers on the Thames for well over a century. Here, the post-war *Royal Sovereign* sails past Gravesend on 29 July 1964.

The tugs *Dhulia* (left) and *Hibernia* (right) sail up river on 26 August 1964. Tugs were a common sight in the river at Gravesend, awaiting vessels coming up river, where they would needs tugs to dock in the various wharves and docks.

The MV *Sagafjord* was built in France for the Norwegian America Line in 1965 and ended her career with Saga as the *Saga Rose*, after a period with Cunard.

In 1966 and 1967, the ex-Clyde paddler *Jeanie Deans* sailed on the Thames as the *Queen of the South*. She is shown here on 11 June 1966 at the start of her maiden season on the Thames.

Ships at Gravesend, 3 March 1967. In view are the Greek MV *Nymphe* and the MV *Rogate*, as well as three tugs and a solitary fishing boat.

The Swedish MV *Hispania* (8,554grt, built 1966) off Gravesend on 3 June 1971.

The Greek emigrant ship SS *Regina Magna* (32,360grt, built 1938) on another 'Ten Pound Pom' voyage off Gravesend on 23 June 1972. She had begun her career as the French *Pasteur* and had sailed as the *Bremen* for North German Lloyd. On tow to the breakers she sank in the Indian Ocean.